Also includes strategies to start your
2nd Income with Zero investments

Also includes strategies to start your 2nd Income with Zero investments

THE SECRETS OF MONEY MASTERY

YOGENDRA SHAH

Worldwide Published by

Pendown Press

PENDOWN PRESS

An ISO 9001 & ISO 14001 Certified Co.,

Regd. Office: 2525/193, 1st Floor, Onkar Nagar-A,
Tri Nagar, Delhi-110035

Ph.: 09350849407, 09312235086

E-mail: info@pendownpress.com

Branch Office: 1A/2A, 20, Hari Sadan, Ansari Road,
Daryaganj, New Delhi-110002

Ph.: 011-45794768

Website: PendownPress.com

First Edition: 2020

ISBN: 978-93-90116-71-3

Layout and Cover Designed by Pendown Graphics Team

Printed and Bound in India by Thomson Press India Ltd.

CONTENTS

Testimonials vi

Preface vii

Acknowledgements ix

1. Why I am writing this book? 1
2. Two Ways: To Become Wealthy 9
3. Whom this book will help the most? 11
   - (a) You Struggle with your Little Money 11
   - (b) Your Money does not Multiply 17
   - (c) How will Money help? I am Not Sure!! 25
4. THE BIGG Problem!! 29
5. Mistakes that Smart Investors Make 33
6. **The Turnaround solution to Money Woes:** Step by step framework to create your 2nd income 43
   - (a) **Principle 1:** Build Your Own Money Printing Assets. 47
   - (b) **Principle 2:** Capitalize on Third Party Assets. 50
7. Conclusion is always a new beginning 55

TESTIMONIALS

"Don't forget to read this book before you invest your next dime."

–Gaurav Tripathi
Business Development Manager (India), Johnson Control

"I had been really insensible with my Money. This book is an eye opener."

–Siddharth Banerjee
Serial Entrepreneur, Solution Design Architect,
Ex. Reliance Retail, Huawei, Samsung,

"This book gives you some great ideas to start your 2nd income, even if you do not have any assets. Thanks, Yogendra for these insights."

–Rupesh Singh
Chief Officer, Merchant Navy

PREFACE

This book highlights key investing blunders that most investors make. These blunders prevent them from achieving their lives' dreams and desires. **A negative approach towards money destroys your hard-earned assets.** This happens to be the key reason why people have a constant struggle with money and how just by tweaking their attitude towards Money, they can have it in abundance. The book also highlights the fact: why even wealthy find themselves on the wrong side of Money? **Most importantly,** you will find in it how to develop **Money Mastery and stress-free life** by creating a parallel regular income flow **even if you do not have any assets.**

ACKNOWLEDGEMENTS

It is easier said than done. Composing this book was a bigger struggle than I thought initially. It took me over 5 months to reach to this finish line and procrastination took over ambition many times. But I can tell you with absolute certainty, the reward and sense of success is much higher than all the pain.

I thank entire team of Pendown Press (Publisher of this book) for their constant support and motivation. An incredibly special thanks to my friend and Mentor Akshar Yadav for handholding me through this beautiful book writing journey.

I feel blessed to be at the helm of my Advisory Firm (SNMA) and gratitude to all our wonderful customers who have been with us in this journey.

I cannot miss to thank my wife Rati and childhood friend Satendra Mahara, who chipped in their wisdom on several aspects of the book and have constantly motivated me.

Chapter-1

WHY I AM WRITING THIS BOOK?

Money is the most important thread in our life. We work for it whole life, sacrifice everything, including our passions. We compromise to the highest order, just to have that bank balance and Money in our pockets, but what MOST fail to understand is the relationship that we share with Money.

We never spend time to understand why Money matters to us and how having it in abundance, will solve the problems of life.

"Money is the medium of Exchange, and that is its paramount function. But this is not the concept we follow."

Every individual enjoys a distinct relationship with Money. It happens to be the single biggest factor for our motivation and right from birth, we start preparing and programming ourselves to attain

Money in Abundance. The desire and quest for Money can be understood from single fact that 70% of our lives' activities and act are singularly targeted to fetch More Money.

Therefore, no one will doubt why Money happens to be the single most contributor to our stress, when we fail to attain the desired amount. Apparently, **most of our tasks culminate in attainment of Money.**

You go to school to acquire knowledge on Money; how best can you contribute to a system (business) to get monetary compensation for your time. Or at best, you get seasoned to run a Business and trade off with Money in return.

How we acquire Money, path we choose to access it, how we manage and spend Money, all these largely depend on the following factors:

(a) **Value and Education,** you have received on Money during childhood: from family, friends, and circle of influence.

(b) How have you **organised this information mentally?**

(c) How you **pursue Money and how much insecure,** lack of money makes you feel?

(d) How much **Frugal or Extravagant** you are?

(e) Is it **a matter of pride,** or you take it as an outcome of your efforts in addressing a problem?

Every individual process and organizes Money messages uniquely and develop certain automatic pattern with which it treats Money. These are known as **Money Habits.**

In the Past 16 years, I managed Money & created wealth for over 2000 individual and over 200 institutions, all coming from different walks of life, different life stages, varying aspirations, and Money needs. But a desire within me remains unanswered; **The desire to transform people's relationship with Money.**

The BIGGEST realization for me in these 16 Years was **that returns on investments which every investor chase, is largely insignificant and more of psychological than an underlying need.**

Let me prove this statement.

- Investors crave for high returns to have more **Money, but they remain unsure of what value this so-called more Money from High returns is creating for them. They do not have**

measured end goals to meet from More Money?

- High returns come from owning highly volatile assets. Can you bear the pain? Love it or hate it. This is the reality. Do you sharpen your tools before the game?
- What happiness every single percent increase in returns will bring, **or how bad and depressed will you feel, if you do not get it?**

> *"Fear and Greed are the emotions responsible for most of our mistakes."*
>
> ***–Yogendra Shah***

Pragmatically, there is no definition of HIGH Returns. It is only to the tune of one's ability to absorb losses. Logically, there is no urgent need of high returns till you do not have measured goals to meet. Investors do not even know how to reach there because it has never been measured. Also, they are clueless on how much every single Unit of Higher risk taken, is taking them closer to a defined objective.

Investors' Agony: A sales representative walks up with a promise, and you are quickly lured because all you have thought is "HIGH RETURNS" wherein some **simple investing strategies** serve the purpose. You do not even know where exactly this new bee (high return product) will fit in, how will it impact your overall returns, what extra high risk it brings along, and you indulge in, because you get blinded with high returns, which never comes without a strategy.

Wealth Destruction: Leveraged Stock Trading is one of the most merciless ways of destroying wealth. Few investors end up making money initially and then eventually start denting their capital, and for many, entire capital is wiped off.

Psychology has a major role here. It becomes difficult to say **'No'** to something alluring. And this desire gets intense when stock markets are doing good and everyone is making Money. Fear of Missing out (FOMO) kicks in.

Face the Reality: The Sole Purpose Investing is to ensure that:

1. In rainy days, you have enough funds to sustain.

2. It takes care of your family needs and aspirations.
3. It helps you meet cash flows in at all your financial milestones.
4. **Retirement Security:** You have enough cash flows to manage your aspired retirement. You have continued access to the lifestyle you have always dreamt of.

> *"42% of American investors don't know how their assets are allocated in portfolio- Prudent investment retirement preparedness survey."*

Not knowing what an asset is, like not knowing the braking and acceleration system of the car you are driving. Simply, **an asset is something of value and which appreciates over a period and delivers appreciation higher than inflation.**

> *"Risk comes from not knowing what you are doing."*
>
> ***–Warren Buffet***

We all are tuned to the music of becoming rich, and this music makes us deaf to most warnings in life, whether it is investment, business, or career. This quest to **Get Rich Fast** lures investors to one of the most difficult waters where failure is a near certainty.

"A dear friend of mine Himanshu Sharma (name changed), abjectly criticises share markets, swear on it, calls it "rigged, fake Money, manipulated and a bunch of tricksters running the show". For him, it is the surest and quickest way to destroy wealth. I always took it as a jest, however on probing deep, he once revealed that he punted on share markets with college tuition fee way back in 2001. He gained in some early trade, kept on daring to make bigger leveraged trades and eventually blew all his 2nd year Graduation fee in share markets in less than 35 days.

BOOM. All gone. Brat in business, which he hardly understands. Reason: wanted to have good times with that extra money. Being a BCOM student does not make him an expert in Markets, rather even best of analysts, at times, gets puzzled with Markets' mood swings. And now, what better can he do than to blame it to the markets?

Himanshu started trading after being influenced by his uncle's success stories of making fortune in Trading. Greed Crept in, and it led to massive disappointment. There is no way to make quick Money from the markets without a strategy and Risk Appetite. And no one can make, let me assure you.

All these situations arise from lack of understanding of Money, Value, Price and Patience. (MVPP)

These are pearls of Wisdom which most do not understand and because of ignorance if fortune visits them, they are unable to retain it.

Chapter-2

TWO WAYS TO BECOME WEALTHY

We dream of wealth, abundance, and happiness whole of our life, but there is basic understanding which we miss. This is the sage advice which has got wealth to all wealthy and without this wealth will always give us a miss.

1. **Be in Business and make it large.**
2. **Prudently buy others' Business with shared dreams and aspirations.**

And when I say buy others' businesses, I clearly mean to own their equity, and that is what share market is for. Shares are not just mere piece of reflection in De-mat account, **it is a commitment to marry those businesses which are residing in De-mat account,** a commitment of shared values, aspirations, objectivity and vision of that company's management.

Warren Buffet, Peter Lynch, John Templeton, Rakesh Jhunjhunwala, and scores of other legendary investors were in love with the businesses they owned and were committed to hold them despite any turbulence. When we read things well, we understand them well for being a perfect match.

What we see around, everything is business. To make more money we either lend or partner a business. Banks, which give us a fixed interest on Fixed Deposit is also a business house which borrows in form of FD at low rates and lends to others at higher rates, thus making profit. Banks lends home loans but they always operate out of rented premises.

> *"Build Assets, don't*
> *Multiply your liabilities."*
>
> ***–Yogendra Shah***

Chapter-3

WHOM THIS BOOK WILL HELP THE MOST?

A. You struggle with the little Money you have.

B. Your Money does not Multiply. *(A constant struggle with money growth.)*

C. How will Money help? I am Not Sure!!

A. You struggle with the little Money you have.

> *"It's not how much Money you make, but how much Money you keep, how hard it works for you and how many generations you keep for it."*
>
> ***–Robert Kiyo Saki***

Your Relationship with Money: First Money lesson is learnt at home; we pick it from our parents and people we have grown up with. Go down the memory lane to recall what Money Habits you learnt from them, when you were just growing up, say when you were 6 to 12 years old. **Recall your first interaction with Money.**

- Whether you were told **how to Manage Money properly,**
- How to keep an account book,
- **How to track your spending,** how not to overspend,
- How to utilize Money in the best possible way for gratification.

OR

Hardship about Money was served, and you grew up with chants of **'it is so difficult to earn'.** 'You should not be spending at all'. Stories of your parent's Money struggle was the only thing you remember.

Now we need to understand that these childhood lessons become the part of our core memory and our brain functions are tuned accordingly. We receive, interpret and process information accordingly. **A child who has lived in scarcity and was always told Money is difficult, processes information accordingly and tends to struggle with Money.**

Well, I'm not debating on upbringing, or advocating that one should show false abundance to child, but the basic Money management skills need to be instilled in a child whether he gets Rs 100/- a month or Rs 10,000/- a month as pocket money. A discipline, **do's, and don'ts with Money** needs to be taught in early years.

I have come across scores of young working professionals, who are working for last 0-5 year/s, earning a respectable salary, but surprisingly many of them go broke by 15th of the Month. And they start borrowing to survive the next 15 days. On salary day, their priority is not to invest and create wealth for future but to clear their debts, more than half of the salary goes on that very salary day, clearing casual borrowings, forget any budgeting or savings. This is a vicious cycle. **A DEBT TRAP.** By the time one is out from this, he would have wasted precious early years of investing.

On the contrary, I have a maid working in our residential society. One of the most punctual females, she does her work with absolute ethics and responsibility. She works tirelessly, always wears a smile on her face and interestingly, most other maids are jealous of her. **Can you guess the reason?**

She is amongst very the few maids, or probably the only one in the condominium, who owns a home nearby. House is not important here, what is to be factored in is that she draws the same salary what other maids get, works probably in lesser number of apartments, her husband humbly runs a battery-driven rickshaw and they were not fortunate with any windfall or lottery. Then how did she manage to own a home while no other maid could do it?

She answers this with confidence, "Since we got married some 35 years back, we always dreamt of having our own home and hence we planned and saved for it. Her two bank accounts and banking knowledge is testimony of this. She is privy of basic banking and makes regular Fixed Deposits. **Essentially, she knows what savings is and how to make Money from Money to fulfill her aspirations.** And most importantly, she aspires and is clear on what she wants to achieve in life.

> *"You will never attain your Money Goals till you set it and mentally rehearse it."*
>
> ***–Yogendra Shah***

And in stark contrast, most people part away with Money to acquire liabilities. Fancy phones, gadgets, other expensive stuff, you name it and we need it. Further what is disastrous is, we mostly don't buy these objects because it is needed and we just cannot do without it, but this is to satiate an addiction to possess objects to prove to the community and to create self-importance. And the reality is- people are least interested in what you own, they only look at what benefits you can offer to them.

Little do people know, whenever you shop, big or small, it gives you a sense of accomplishment, a small high, a dopamine hit in your brain and this is the reason you want to repeat that behavior apart from any buying necessities. This loop is never ending, you want to possess stuff, and get binging for your mental satisfaction, to show off to people around, and to further compound this addiction, in today's generation you don’t need to visit the store, it's all at a click of button.

You are constantly bombarded with subtle marketing, which will chase you everywhere, like a precision guided target locked missile, till the purchase is made. It requires awareness and courage to stay unshaken on your course.

This irresistible addiction to Acquire LIABILITIES pushes you into a vicious loop where you further start building liabilities (loans) to get rid of earlier liabilities (say, paying credit card bills). Budgeting your expense and allocating funds for specific spends needs lots of discipline. And this is rarely practiced.

A suggestion to my readers: Make your expense list and question yourself:

- Which are the items you do not need?
- Which are those purchases you can downgrade and will be equally happy with their lower versions?
- Highlight the purchase which was a pure flaunt.

Write back to us to get a copy of Expense Mastery worksheet. yogendra@yogendrashah.com

B. Your Money does not Multiply.

Most investors assume, investing is a number game and they just chase returns. But sadly, the truth is, Wealth Creation is a detailed Goal Setting, Orchestrating a strategy and pure game of psychology.

> *"Your ability to get higher returns is equal to your tolerance of temporary downsides on Assets."*
>
> ***–Yogendra Shah***

A Quick Hack for You

Investment Narration	Option 1	Option 2	Option 3
Capital Invested	50K	5 Million	50 Million
Loss Incurred.	10K	1 Million	10 Million
Loss%	-20%	-20%	-20%

Pick up a situation you would like to be in from above options, considering each also gives an opportunity to make 40 percent positive returns as well. All 3 are identical scenarios. **A 20 Percent loss or chance 40 percent gains,** but quantum of your exposure differs. You might be ok with the same 20 Percent loss in Option 1, but it can rattle you in Option 2 and devastate you in Option 3. **That is how psychology plays. Risk Tolerance is subjective to the portion of wealth you are putting in Volatility.**

"I vividly remember 2008 financial markets meltdown, during Global Financial Crisis. This gentleman happened to be the CEO (India) of a Fortune 500 company, based in Noida, and in the last 3-4 years, he stacked majority of his wealth in Equities as he enjoyed one of the best runs of Equity markets. Then, it was absolute panic in early 2008 when gradual market meltdown started. In the first few months of 2008, hopes held high, but post official declaration of

Lehman Brothers collapse, markets were doomed, investors took it as end of road, we would never see top Wall Street banks rattle so badly. Most investors including him panicked, choose to incur losses, and moved out of Equities. I was working with ABN AMRO Bank that time and our entire senior management was there to assure him of this temporary phase of the market. But anxiety was high and he sold his holdings at -41 percent losses, only to realize two years later, what blunder had he made.

Did you invest in equities in 2008? I would love to know your reaction and more importantly, how did you manage that phase? Please do write back to me and share your experiences and also to get a bonus gift from us. My contact details will be at the end of the book.

Behavioral Economics points out that all of us tend to be susceptible to psychological biases. We tend to overweight recent evidence, especially evidence that are negative, a lot more than evidences of importance.

Fear kicked in 2008-09, media was constantly pounding every single hour, how bad things are going to be. **We tend to give up hope when investing fundamentals are not strong, strategy is not in place and Assets are not evenly divided.** And history has it, markets made a strong come back sooner, but patience and faith gives up every time. This is not a unique case study. I find every third investor with such reckless mindset. **No goal setting, hence, no goal getting.**

The fundamental problem lies in the core of investing. The biggest mistake that investors make is investing basis, some recent media articles, or some glossy Star Ratings. Media and data on Artificial Intelligence enabled research websites only highlight the past performance and it is no assurance that it will continue to perform, until current critical economic conditions are factored it. Investors are lured into it, expecting good days to continue. It goes good till the time markets are performing. But, the moment economy hits a roadblock and downturn starts, Asset prices take a beating. Investors can play brave to some extent but if bad news continues, **faith is shattered**. Media get flooded with how bad economy is going to be and what worse is in store. Naysayers are on prowl. It is difficult to show courage and hold on to your position.

And this situation is exactly opposite to basic of all investment philosophies. **Good assets are the best to buy when they are getting sold at dirt cheap price,** when everyone is dumping them. And this can only happen when there is a strategy in place.

You can change the entire narrative by choosing the basics, the rock-solid framework of investing, by framing your question, right? What are your goals and desires, and **how you want your Money to perform to help you reach those goals?** 'It is critical that your answer your '**How, Which & What**' correctly.

- **How do I attain my financial goals and objectives?**
- **Which Assets will help me reach there?**
- **What Asset Allocation strategy will take me there?**

Wealthy gets Wealthier: What makes Wealthy a **Money Magnet,** is their Mindset. They are totally immune to market noises; they understand their risk capital and make the biggest Money out of Asset Crashes. They love buying Assets at dirt cheap prices, are extremely rationale in their approach, and not driven by emotions. On the contrary, 95% of Retail Investor dump their assets in crashes and come back when markets bounce back. The reason is: **Herd mentality,** they just got to know that their neighbor made some good Money out of stocks. No research, no data digging, no professional advice, just influence.

Vulture Funds: Vulture fund is a good example of distressed buying. In developed markets, an investment fund which seeks to invest in **extremely distressed Assets is called a Vulture Fund.** And they end up making a killing of it. They buy bonds, equities of companies that are near bankrupt. The goal is to 'swoop in' and pick up under-priced shares that are perceived to have been oversold to make high-risk, but potentially high-reward bets.

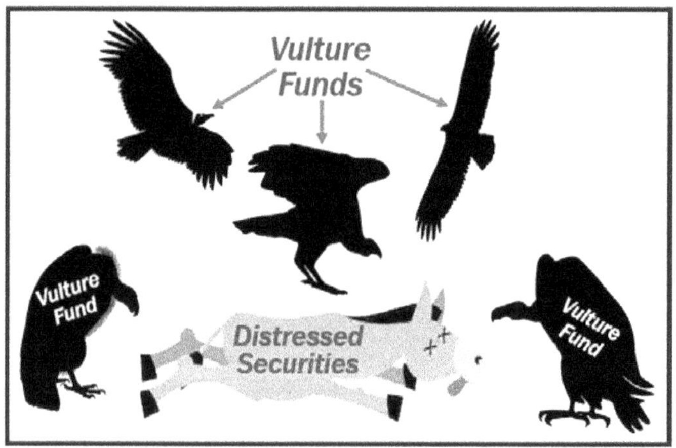

> *"Buy when there's blood in the streets, even if the blood is your own."*

This is a quote by **Baron Rothschild**, an 18th-century British nobleman, who made a fortune by buying in panic. But this philosophy of buying cheap and selling expensive is rarely followed.

> *"Be in the Right asset at the right time."*
>
> ***–Yogendra Shah***

Wealth is Subjective, perception of wealth differs from person to person. But what remains the same is the psychology of Asset creation. **Earning high does not makes one wealthy.** You create wealth when you know the **science of Asset Creation,** when you are constantly building assets from your income.

Those higher earners who do not understand principles of asset creation and Money Management become examples of **RICHES to RAGS.**

On his third 20th Birthday *(that is how he loved addressing his 60th Birthday)* **Indian failed Business**

Tycoon Vijaya Mallya flew in Spanish pop singer Enrique Iglesias to Goa for his Birthday Celebrations. It was a brazen display of wealth even when he owed over INR 9000 Crore to Indian Banks. From Multimillion Dollar private yacht to fancy Jets, he had it all which called for his doom. Apart from failed business, his extravagant lifestyle and spending failed Vijaya Mallya. And the list doesn't end here, be it **Hollywood Star Johnny Depp, or Boxer Mike Tyson or even King of Pop Michael Jackson** who supposedly had $400 Million Debt, when he died in 2009, they were extremely successful in their career, made fortune, but their lifestyle failed them and they went broke.

> *"Do not tell me where your priorities are. Show me where you spend your Money and I will tell you what they are."*
>
> ***–James W. Frick***
> *Former vice president for public relations, alumni affairs, and development at the University of Notre Dame*

- Are you extravagant and spend more than it is needed?

- Do you love flaunting your possessions and think that is the only way you can prove it to others that you have arrived?

If your answer to these questions are YES, we can help you. Write back to access a step by step framework to gain control on your spending's.

C. How will Money help? I am Not Sure!!

May 2019, a south Delhi based business family approached us. They were in utter chaos with multiple defaults happening in their Debt Mutual funds and private company bonds that they held. In over exuberance, they piled up high Yield Bonds & Debt MFs in last 2 years, now in deep crisis, they were unable to figure out whether they should exit at losses or continue holding. All they did was to sit with bated breath, catching news of carnage in debt markets every single month. Anxiety built up, and indecisions prevailed. Not convinced with their Bank's Wealth Management team, who advised them to invest in these, they actively scouted for some professional, for unbiased advice. And mind you, this was not an old investment, in just last 24 months, they did this all.

My first question to them was Point Blank. Why did you expose such a large portion of your hard-earned Money in these risky assets? Since 2018, after ILFS default, bond markets were extremely risky. What was the point of taking this additional risk? You invest in Fixed Income to have certainty of returns and peace of mind. And now if you are prompted to visit your investments every single day, something was not right.

My questions to them were precise:

- What reward was expected with this high risk taken?
- How this extra 1%-2% returns was helping them?
- What goals and end objective were earmarked against this reward?
- Was this extra 1%-2% addressing any of the financial gaps, or just a psychological trap?
- If this was your risk capital, then why not a calculated exposure to other Assets and target 5% higher returns?

Unfortunately, they had answers to none. Reckless investing, no Asset Allocation, just lured to high returns.

We did a stress test on all their Funds & Securities. Booking losses is always painful, but it is better to get out now at 20% loss rather than having to write off that entire investments later. We held back 65% of the assets where there was bright chances of recovery and rest were sold at varying discounts. As I write today, it has been 11 months since we did this exercise, the **Assets we have retained has appreciated by 16.7%.** This includes some recoveries from few of the delinquent companies. And from past 3 months, we have been constantly shifting these funds to other Safest Assets, for a remarkably high safety of capital.

Many times, you must look at **RETURN OF CAPITAL** and not only on **RETURN's ON CAPITAL.**

Our relationship with Money is complex and mostly not understood. The mad rush for Money is one of the reasons that we have not attributed any definition or purpose to Money. It is important to be aware and mindful of what harmony Money brings to you to sustain your life's priorities, success of business or work you indulge in.

We have designed an unshakable framework to create an incredibly Safe Fixed Income Portfolio, which is extremely tax efficient. Write back to us to at **yogendra@yogendrashah.com** *do get your dream fixed income, every month.*

Chapter-4

THE BIGG PROBLEM!!

In current challenging environment, riddled with constant job losses, rising unemployment, tepid salary growth, stagnant businesses, only **one thing is certain, our ever- increasing expense, constant desire to upgrade our living status, renovate our homes, get hold of the latest gadget, cars, accessory, exotic vacations and the desire for newer, better, smarter, fancier lifestyle and objects is ever growing.** Either we are tuned to this music or get ourselves tuned through our family members, peers, friends, colleagues, and media. Everyone seems to be so influencing. All these factors lead to a **Money Crisis.**

Even worst, we are aware of these challenges, but have never made a conclusive strategy to deal with them, a strategy where Money will never be a problem.

- We never tried spending awareness.
- Strategy to detach from spending addictions.

- Never traced where money is flowing out.
- Tried finding replacement to large expense.
- Created strategy to clear off debt.
- Strategy to tackle an unforeseen future earning loss.
- **Before mid age, we never tested having a parallel income which is higher than our Monthly expenses, and now we are bound to meet Midlife crisis.**

A **Midlife crisis** is a transition of identity and self-confidence that can occur in middle-aged individuals, typically 45 to 55 years old. The phenomenon is described as a psychological crisis brought about by events that highlight a person's growing age, inevitable mortality, and possibly lack of accomplishments and proper finances in life. This may produce feelings of intense depression, remorse, and high levels of anxiety, or the desire to achieve youthfulness or make drastic changes to their current lifestyle or feel the wish to change past decisions and events. (Wikipedia)

Chapter-5

MISTAKES THAT SMART INVESTORS MAKE

Clarity on your Financial Milestones: Clarity First, this is also title of a book written by a friend, and I deeply appreciate it. Absolute clarity leaves little room for confusion and disorder. It helps you set in a clear, visible, actionable roadmap for your **Financial Freedom.**

You will be surprised to know this: **The biggest blunder most investors make is:** and I do not mince my words, this conclusion is a result of over 1,000 interactions that I had with different individuals who hail from different walks of life, social and financial strata.

- 76% of them are **clueless on their Financial Milestones.**
- **Over 90% do not do a goal-based investing.** And hold on, this is even though they very well

understand financial jargons like retirement planning, children's higher education, but they do not budget, do not invest as per asset allocation and no annual recalibration of milestone.

Only one thing that rules their mind and life is **HIGH RETURNS** and assumptions that my piece of land, or the stocks lying in the De-mat account will help take care of retirement or child's higher education.

Well, the reality is that no asset or business has a perpetual growth, it peaks at a point and then decline begins if it is not managed well. Journey from being wealth creators to Wealth Destroyers, is always swift.

Pitfalls you will fall in while investing

A. **Lack of Product Information:** It is tragic with many 'do it yourself' (DIY) investors, a quick browsing, short historical performance check, or a recent newspaper article about some Assets performance is enough for them to pounce on it. No one tries to read in between the lines, analyze the historic returns in various phases, peer comparison and future growth analysis.

Past performance is no certainty that it will be repeated in future. Right assets must get identified when it is not in news, by the time it is in media, it is overpriced.

B. **You Dabble in Stocks for Quick Money:** Perfect recipe for disaster. There is nothing like quick and easy Money. Even the most coveted traders lose many of their trades. Never try to know the depth of river with both feet. If at all you do, earmark your risk capital, educate yourself before you even think of doing it and most importantly, take professional help.

C. **You are too conservative:** Great Savers are foolish investors. **They forget the basic principle of economics that the one who has borrowed, will make more of the Money of lender.** Consider this: You will borrow money at 10% for your business only if you know that funds can be utilised in a way that it helps you fetch at least 11% or more.

When we make Fixed Deposit in a bank, we lend it to a business, bank further lends it to deserving borrowers who make more from our money, bank also makes money from our money and returns us a piddle little interest. And don't forget, government also tax you on this, because government knows you are trying to make Money while sleeping and government also have to safeguard your interest (the entire transaction) through RBI, so it penalizes you with higher tax. Fixed deposits do not even beat inflation, the basic premise of investing.

Here I am not indicating Fixed deposits as an inferior investment, but it should be part of Asset Allocation Strategy, not the strategy itself to just make Fixed Deposits.

D. **You Love Liabilities:** Your intimacy with spending defines your financial success. No matter how high you earn, if you get carried away with spending addictions, fall is round the corner.

> *"That man is richest whose pleasure are cheapest."*
>
> ***–Henry David Thoreau***
> *American Philosopher*

E. **You do not invest enough.** There is no one size that fits all. Invest with a purpose, for a dream, for an aspiration, and for a milestone. When the goals are defined, expectations are set, vision is clear, investing regularly becomes easy. Just do not toss off few thousand in monthly SIPs or in some lousy insurance policy and proclaim victory.

> *"Do not save what is left after spending; instead, spend what is left after saving."*
>
> ***–Warren Buffet***

F. **You Never Follow Science of Asset Allocation:** Mindless investing is nothing short of self-sabotage. **Asset Allocation plays a critical role in Binding Risk and returns in right proportion.** This is the only failproof strategy that helps investor seek the most optimal reward from investing. It helps you reach the objectivity of your investments. **Right Asset allocation is the single most CRITICAL factor for your investment success.**

Asset means anything of value which appreciates over a period. Real Assets should appreciate well over inflation so that you get Real Returns.

Asset Allocation is the process of allocating investments in different Assets which will help you reach your investment objective. A simple process, but rarely followed. Rather, let me be frank, it is a rarity to see to any investor following these investment basics:

- ✓ **Investment Objective.**
- ✓ **Time Horizon.**
- ✓ **Risk Tolerance.**
- ✓ **Asset Allocation.**
- ✓ **Appropriate Bench marking.**
- ✓ **Accurate product selection.**

G. **Tax is an expense:** Till the time you do not tag tax as an expense and strategize meticulously to minimize, it will continue to suck out major portion from your earnings. But investors never treat it as an expense, it is a hard reality with which one must live with and should actively plan to lessen the impact.

It does not stop at your income levels, but every time your tax paid income generates further income, taxes further eat a pie of it, if not strategized to minimize it. There is no way it can be completely skipped, but for sure one can lessen its impact.

H. **You are Loaded with Junk Assets:** It is by-product of senseless investing. Greed and expectation of high returns rule supreme when you buy it. What lacked was the rationale- No exit strategy. Emotions play hard, fear stops you from parting with them when in distress. With Junk in kitty any further opportunity to invest in good assets is also lost. And worse, it acquires most of your mental space.

> *"Tactics without strategy is the noise before defeat."*
>
> ***–Sun Tzu***
>
> *Chinese Military Strategist & Philosopher*

I met Mr. Talreja, a Gurgaon based businessman in 2017. That year share markets were exuberant, any pick would fetch instant returns, within days. Stock trading became his primary business. Not that he was making great Money, but daily success in stocks gave him that HIGH, the Dopamine rush, which everyone craves for. We began with managing his other funds as stock market was very dear to him and he wanted to manage it on his own. Still as an advisory partner, we gave a stern indication to be wary of such market trading. **"This addiction can be the death of Wealth Creation"**. Earmark your risk capital and use that only for daily trades. But who would heed to wisdom when daily addictions are ruling high?

The **biggest truth** is no one loves any assets, be it Fixed deposits, real estate or equities. We just love More Money, More Returns, Higher the returns an asset seem to be fetching, more attracted we are towards it. And daily trading is also the next level of addiction; it depicts similar behavioral patterns of gaming addicts or gamblers.

2018 onwards, hell broke loose on Mr. Talreja's Stock holdings. His stock holdings initially tanked -10 percent till almost a blood bath of -47percent returns by mid-2019. He could not even get sense and courage to recalibrate his investments, utter chaos and confusion prevailed. I used to get frantic calls from him explaining his situation and what should he do.

Finally, he requested us to get him out of this mess. Initially, I was zapped to see his unending stock portfolio of over 52 stocks. Every script was complex to understand, under what circumstance were these bought. What study was behind investing in it. After a painful one week of analysis and scrubbing his holding through various growth parameters, we squeezed the list of stocks to 18. Further, it was exceedingly difficult to convince him to book loss on few where there were no chances of recovery.

We just cannot get into direct stocks without any stop losses. Few businesses will always phase out eventually and we hold it on expecting a recovery, which rarely happens, if your research is not right. They become Wealth Destroyers.

By Jan 2020 beginning, we further squeezed down the bunch of stocks to 14. By then he was also able to recover 65 percent of the losses, as we reinvested in strong performing, evergreen brands. Full recovery should take some time as advent of lockdown due to corona virus has further impacted the portfolio, but now we are not worried. We know where we have invested, pedigree of the businesses we own and certain of the fact that these businesses will bounce back.

Chapter-6

THE TURNAROUND SOLUTION TO MONEY WOES

Step by Step Framework to Start Your Second Income

As human being we constantly yearn for Safety and Security, we constantly scouts for options to protect us, to keep us safe, to survive and thrive, and to also have a desired lifestyle. We might have varying fancies and desires, but in the background, we all vibrate at the same frequency—the frequency of stability, of comfort, and predictability. We venture out, take risk only to bring back more certainty.

We at times hate what we do, but we drag, what makes us passionate mostly remains away from us, because our work commitment prevents us from pursuing those passions. And all this is because we want to continue to run our household, pay those recurring monthly bills, sustain our expenses. The pain grows deeper if we have only one source of income flowing in, only one avenue to look up every month, month-on-month. If that dries up, we are choked and this feeling of being choked, chokes us every day. **This is the major contributor for our daily Stress, the Financial Stress.**

> *"Never depend on single income, make investments to create second."*
>
> **–Warren Buffet**
> *Legendary Investor*

This is one super solution to most of our woes. This is the mechanism that can dilute massive stress we deal every single day. The mechanism which will help you create a parallel income which is higher than your monthly expense, so that you follow your passion, without worrying about the monthly bills.

The mechanism is simple, but rarely followed. A system which everyone needs, be it king or popper. Unfortunately, the general notion is to plan for second income when we retire, but it should be planned on the very day we got our first salary or at the onset of the business we are in.

A parallel source of income which could take care of all your ever-increasing monthly expenses is critical and, now I will make it as simple as A, B, C.

Characteristics of your Second Income: It should be

- Automatic.
- More than your monthly expenses.
- Increase with ongoing inflation.
- Allow you to sustain the lifestyle you always dreamt of.
- Give some headroom for luxury.
- The sooner it starts better it is, so that you have time for epic things in life, as magic happens when you start following your passion.

And believe me, this all is attainable. If you can think of it, it can be strategized and attained. All that it needs is education, expert guidance, strategic planning, and careful implementation.

For ease, I am listing down the step by step procedure to get your second income going:

1. Write down your number (monthly expense) for second income. How much is needed now to run your family happily?
2. Adjust it for ever-increasing inflation.
3. Take professional help in creating an Asset Allocation.
4. Choose appropriate investment instruments. Let us say for Equities as an Asset, which fund or Stocks will help in your regular monthly income flow. It is the most crucial part of investing where most mistakes occur. Do educate yourself right, else best is to seek professional help.
5. Choose a deadline for execution.
6. **Do Remember:** Tax Optimization can change the game.

Below are some of the Top options which will support you for regular cash flows.

Principle 1: Build your Own Money Printing Assets

OPTION 1:

High Dividend Paying Stocks: From stock market universe, if carefully picked, investors can tailor make a Bouquet of High dividend Yielding stocks which can potentially fetch you 3%-5% Dividend Yield, plus an above average growth.

One needs to be actively involved in cherry picking and weed out as valuations rises. With recent tax changes, in which dividend in the hand of investors is taxable, do check whether this option is viable for you or not.

OPTION 2:

Equity Mutual Fund SWP: Systematic Withdrawal Plans have not gained much popularity as a tool of regular income flow. Though **it happens to be one of the most potent tool** for regular withdrawal of funds to meet your expenses, be it any Asset Class in Mutual

Funds, SWPs can help you make calculated withdrawals.

OPTION 3:

Commercial Real Estate: Acquiring a high-yielding Commercial space is a traditionally accepted practice. Do your math's well. 7%-9% Rental Yield and clear visible capital appreciation is a must.

OPTION 4:

REITS: Real estate investment trust. Though a fairly new concept in India, but a great option for those who lack the quantum of funds needed to own a good retail / office space.

Like mutual funds, the underlying asset in REIT is physical rental yielding, income generating real estate.

OPTION 5:

Sovereign State/Central Govt. Bonds: These bonds are issued by Central govt. PSU, State Govt. and carry top safety. They yield higher than a Bank FD and are considered safe. The attraction is their periodical interest payments.

OPTION 6:

Peer to Peer Lending: It is gaining popularity. It is a process of lending Money directly to borrower and eliminating intermediaries like banks/NBFCs. You can choose the interest rate you want to get after understanding risk associated with it. Higher the return expectation, higher will be the risk.

Many RBI-approved online lending platform offer this service, Faircent was the first to receive permission from RBI and is one of the biggest P2P lenders in India.

OPTION 7:

TAX FREE Bonds: This Zero tax-on-returns investment is the most sought-after instrument for sheer convenience and clarity. Highly popular amongst HNI, Tax free bonds are issued by Govt. enterprises like IRCTC, HUDCO, etc., to raise funds for a specific purpose. They are considered as highly safe as they have Govt's backing. They are tax free as per Section 10 of the Income Tax Act of India, 1961. Time horizon for these bonds is 10 Years, though they can be liquidated in secondary market.

OPTION 8:

Post Office MIP, RBI Bonds: Post office monthly income plan which currently fetches 6.6% is way higher than most frontline banks FDs which are at 5.5% annual Interest. So is RBI's 7 Years' Bond which gets 7.15%.

OPTION 9:

Stock Trading: No child's play, needs lot of discipline and learning, but if mastered it can help you fetch regular income flows. Beware, over 90% of retail traders lose money while trading.

Now, what if you do not have a large sum of money to invest for regular returns? Do not worry, I will help you there as well. You can trade your time by using below hacks to create a regular income without even having a penny to invest.

Principle 2: Capitalize on Third Party Assets:

A. **Sell your Pictures online:** Continue to do what you love to do. Just click good and upload. You may choose portals like **Shutter stock, Adobe stock, iStock, Getty images, SmugMug,** just to name a few. Any and every moment if smartly captured, can fetch you a price. This business is growing rapidly, and the massive demand of pictures is ever- increasing.

B. **Offer online Opinion/Reviews:** Everyone has an opinion, which might not be suitable to many, but can-do wonders to a lot. I remember making a purchase from Amazon; how seller at times chase you for good review. And every single good review pulls hundreds of further sales. It's basically like a consumer telling the world, 'Hey!! Look if you buy books, Seller X is the best, buy it from him. And here starts the trail of influencing buying behavior."

Travel reviews are most sought after; before one travels to a new place, he wants to have a feel of it. And what could be better than getting paid for sharing your experience!

Understand this, you are good in something, have certain experiences and the world is craving for it. You must use the right medium to disseminate your message in a consumable manner. Check for Amazon vine program where Amazon invites some of its trusted reviewers for its new release or pre- release reviews.

C. **Create YouTube Videos:** Just a thought, what if I could have made a nano video of all what I bought in last five years. Just unbox it and give a quick review of how my experience was. Well, I do not have any real count of all what I purchased in last 5 years, but it should be over 250 purchases considering 1 item a week. Consumers are hungry to understand which is the right product for them, they lack decision making, they want to be driven, influenced. You can also do so for a manufacturer and get paid, or just start putting recordings of your personal experiences on YouTube.

D. **Affiliate Marketing:** The **biggest tool to make Money online, without investing a penny.** No special skill set is needed, except basic computer knowledge, a blog and taste to narrate things, compare articles in a manner that it can drive traffic to your affiliated product and a subsequent sale.

   It is basically your affiliation with a product or services, and you market it online in a manner that drives buyers' decision-making behavior, prompts them to visit your affiliate website or page and eventually drive a purchase. You can become **Amazon affiliate** and choose from variety of products and services that they offer. Even I got myself enrolled in Amazon; you lose nothing in writing few reviews of products you genuinely like and you would not mind making some quick bucks on it.

E. **Blogging-Consulting-Education:** Every person is unique and has some great experiences which is worth sharing. We tend to be very prompt in offering free advice even when it is not sought. But, what if you can utilise your knowledge bank and present it in such a way that people would love to pay you for that. Viewers will love to visit your website because they get immense value from it and mind you; advertisers are watching it. They will never shy away from advertising on your blog/website, if you have been able to generate good traffic on it.

F. **Become a Virtual Assistant:** You can do this from the luxury of your home and can choose the hours you want to work. In this, you are remotely assisting a business or a freelancer to complete their tasks, like managing calendar, scheduling their digital marketing activities, managing their personal errand, broadly any task where limited decision making is needed and outsourcing at lower cost makes sense for that business. It also helps businesses, instead of hiring a full-time employee and spending on infra cost; this job can be done by someone sitting in a remote location at a fraction of cost.

Chapter-7

CONCLUSION IS ALWAYS A NEW BEGINNING

This short book is a summary of my 16 years of experience as a banker and a Financial Consultant. It is my learning from over 2,000 investor interactions, their experience with Money and how they perceive money.

Money Mastery is the awareness you have about Money and the relationship you forge with it. While it is natural to think of More Money, but psychologically the thought itself is a stressor and it sabotages your peace and productivity. Start acknowledging Money as tool to attain an experience or object, identify what happiness will they give, strategize and start working towards it.

A little clarity on your Financial Milestone, how and when do you want to achieve objects and experiences can set the tone of your entire Financial Freedom. And once asset creation becomes your passion and you have created parallel income streams, you have attained a Rich Mindset and well set on your journey to prosperity.

To help investors ease their Money stress, we have scientifically designed a Step by step framework to:

- ✓ Develop spending awareness, recalibrate, and shrink your spending.
- ✓ Re-align your existing investments and investing patterns to create a stream of regular income flow, which is higher than your monthly expense.
- ✓ Weed out all your toxic investments.
- ✓ **Turn around** your **laggards to Winners** and create massive Wealth.
- ✓ Reform your taxation.
- ✓ Enjoy up to 20% higher returns on your Fixed Income with same safety.

You can achieve all the above by following our deep researched proven framework. Just drop us an email at **yogendra@yogendrashah.com** and we will get back to help you set free from all you Money worries.

Notes:

www.ingramcontent.com/pod-product-compliance
Ingram Content Group UK Ltd.
Pitfield, Milton Keynes, MK11 3LW, UK
UKHW022007190726
13853UKWH00004B/1787

9 789390 116713